Deise

Dictionary

of

Waterford

Slang

boy!

by Wellboy

www.UpTheDeise.com

for all your Waterford wants and Déise desires...

The Déise Dictionary of Waterford Slang

by Wellboy from UpTheDeise.com

Published by UpTheDeise Enterprises, Waterford, Ireland.

Printing History
December 2006:   First Published Edition

May 2004:   Online Edition on UpTheDeise.com

Visit www.upthedeise.com to purchase the book online, or to contact UpTheDeise Enterprises.

While every precaution has been taken in the preparation of this book, the publisher and author assume no responsibility for errors or omissions, or for damages resulting from the use of the information contained herein.

WARNING: The contents of this book may be offensive or hard to understand for some. This is simply due to the fact that Waterford people may be perceived, due to their dialect, as impolite or hard to understand. Some rude expressions are used in the book in order to accurately and authentically replicate the use of the terms in everyday speech. Often words are spelt phonetically to allow the reader to fully appreciate the ambience of the phrases e.g. "dat ting over dayer boy" translates directly as "that thing over there."

ISBN: 0-9554755-0-3
ISBN13: 978-0-9554755-0-4

Well boy and girl boy!

"Well boy! I fired a chynie from me gallybander at de shellakybooky on dat yungwan's blaa, but I feckin well missed an' she et it anyhow, de feckin daw. I won't be bummin de dogs end offa her now boy, I'd say it tastes cat! She'll have de scutters layter boy, I'n telling ye now!"

If you can read the above paragraph, and understand it, then you are probably from the Déise region. If not, it has been carefully translated for you as follows…

"Hello there sir, I shot a marble from my slingshot at the snail on that young girl's bread roll, however I missed and she ate it nonetheless, the silly person. I definitely shall not be asking her for any of her leftovers now; I imagine they would be very unpalatable indeed! She will have several loose motions in a few hours time my friend, of that I am certain!"

Dis book was compiled by a Waterford yungfella so dat payple can finally understand what us Déise folk are on about. De slang entries are all malojan, so don't come runnin' to us bawlin' if ye tink dey are cat. In fact, butty, if de content of dis book offends ye or ye feel de phrases are mistranslated, go feck off an' shove some red lead in yer roll!

If ye got a loand o' dis copy and ye want to buy wan for yerself, ye can get 'em online on www.upthedeise.com or alternatively in yer local book store.

Finally, if ye wanna know why dis ting was put together in de first place, dayer is only one possible answer boy…

Das de why!!!

Dis book is dedicated tew all de special payple in me life:
de Lack (me luvelly wife),
me little yungwan an' yungfella,
me Faydur, me Muddur,
de rest of me family,
all de in-laws an' outlaws,
an' tew all de lovely payple of de Déise.

A special tanks also goes out tew de followin' few gowlbags for lookin' over dis farce for de good of dayer health (i.e. I told em I'd box de conkers offa dem if dey dihint do what I said):

An Fear Glic
James "Nigsers" Mernin
Conor "Yeronlyman" Ryan
Declan "Breezly" Lawlor
Jonathan "Jay-be-wan" Brazil

Finally, tanks to Waterford writer, Tom Fewer of Callaghane, for all de great advice, which helped to make dis a reality boy!

Notes on using de book

Dictionary Entries

Entries are arranged in alphabetical order and are defined as follows boy:

Word

Class (e.g. n. for noun)
Explanation of word
"Sample Usage"
[synonyms: words with same meaning]

e.g.

Ire (pronounced eye-er)

n.
A rash induced by rubbing together of skin and wet clothing e.g. the inner thighs.
"Yer man must have ire under his arms, his pants are so far up his hole"
[syn: chaffing]

Word Classes:

n.	Noun
v.	Verb
adj.	Adjective
adv.	Adverb
exp.	Expression

A

Anwell
adv.

Without question and beyond doubt.

"Would I g'waffwit yer sister for a scallop boy? Anwell I would!"

All de best
exp.

A farewell remark.

"All de best boy! I better do a legger or I'll get an unmerciful root in de hole offa me muddur for bein' late!"

[syn: G'luck]

Anna Recksick

exp.

In a state of extreme hunger, famished.

*"Quick boy, go out and get me a few crusty blaas.
I'n sick with de hunger and dyin' of anna
recksick."*

Anudder

adj.

Someone or something else.

*"I have fallen for anudder she can make her own
way home!"*

**NOTE: not to be confused with an udder as
that would be manky!**

B

Bangers

n.

Mind altering substances (e.g. red lead).

"I'n telling ye boy, give'm a few worm tablets insteada de bangers, sure he won't know de difference, an' he's always scratchin' his hole anyhow."

Baaieeg (pronounced bah-eeg)

n.

A contrary female.

"Yer wan is some Baaieeg boy! I told her she haves a figure like a sports star but when she asked me 'What sport's star?' I made de mistake of sayin' Eric Bristo and den she bursted me in de mebs!"

Baloney

n.

A meat-like substance only found in West Waterford, not to be confused with the Italian-American meat sausage.

"Jay Mammay, would ye put some baloney in me sangwich today, 'tis wicked like."

[syn: Red Lead]

NOTE to West Waterfordians: Sorry to break this to you like this but the substance you have been calling baloney all these years is actually luncheon sausage (aka red lead)!

Bawling

v.

To shed tears of sadness profusely.

"Yer man was bawling after de slap he got in de bollix. I cried like a baaby meself an I owny cot a glimpse of it boy!

Baytin'

v.

The act of striking or giving blows; punishment or chastisement by blows.

"I gave yer man some baytin' down bunkars hill boy!"

[syn: Yer go]

Bender

n.

A politically incorrect term for a person of homosexual inclination or a person with whom one is not entirely satisfied with.

"I gave yer man some baytin' down slap-arse lane for callin' me a bender!"

Bibe (as gaeilge = Badhb)
n.

A woman who is thoroughly disliked.

"That wan with de hairy face is some bibe boy... I only asked her if she was a yungfella or not an' she et de feckin' head offa me!"

Blaa
n.

A square bread roll of sorts, in one of three varieties: floury, crusty or chewy. The blaa is a culinary delight, unique to Waterford.

"Mammy... make sure you put loads of red lead in me blaa today, dayer wahent a bit in it yesterday an' I was shakin' out in class!"

Blaa Face
n.

An especially hurtful and derogatory comment.

"Get lost ye big blaa face."

The Origin of the Blaa

A Waterford pilgrim (whose name is long since lost) was travelling through de holy land circa 33AD. After many adventures (and misadventures) it just so happened dat he ended up in Jerusalem on de night of de last supper of our Lord. Tired and hungry from all his travels, he came upon an Inn where a small feast was taking place. Being a stranger and with scarcely a few shekels tew his name he decided tew gate crash de party. He hid behind a curtain while de bread was being divided. Craftily he slid one hand out from his hiding place and grabbed a piece of bread. Peter, one of de guests, saw him and grabbed his hand and with an almighty roar declared, "THAT'S BLASPHEMY," to which the Déise boy responded "g'way outa dat boy, dat BLAAS FER ME" and he ran from the room with de sacred bread wrapped up in his blue and white shirt. On returning tew his native Déise he did his best tew reproduce de bread and de closest ting he got tew it was today's famous Waterford Blaa.

And das de truth!!!

- **Tony "Brasscock" McGrath**

Blues (de)

n.

The Waterford United soccer team.

"Well boy, are ye goin' tew see de Blues bayte seven shades of shyte outa dem jackeens dowen in de RSC tonight boy?"

De Blues Chant:
If I had de wings of a swallow,
An' I had de arse of a crow,
I'd fly over [name town] tomorrow,
And shyte on de feckers below.

Bollix

n.

(See Jooks)

NOTE: bollix can also be spelt bollox, however the latter is generally used in a more serious context e.g. "Bollox of a ref!" as opposed to a more light hearted remark such as: "I will in me bollix."

Box

n.

(See Dig)

Buttdur

n.

An oily, unctuous substance obtained from cream by churning.

"Mmmm, have a gawk at dem buttdurry blaas boy!"

Butty

n.

Endearing term used to describe a friend.

"I'll see ye at de match so butty, I'll brin' de Hoppmans boy!"

A sangwich filled with chips.

"Givus chips in me blaa butty dis time girl, an' nuna dat rabbit food nayder!"

Buzz

v.

A feeling of mirth, a joyous state.

"Go on boy, do a penguin for de buzz, just pull your pants down around your ankles, and run up past her house boy."

C

Cabbage Head
n.

A person with an extreme case of irrepressible curly hair.

"Yer man tinks he's de Hoff boy, jus' look at de big cabbage head on him!"

Cake Hole
n.

The mouth or potentially other orifice, depending on context.

"Shut yer feckin' cake hole ye rasher arse!"
[syn: Hole, Gob]

Cannt

v.

The act of losing the central playing apparatus of a game without possibility of retrieval.

"What did you cannt de ball for you feckin' nuitna, now we'll have to use your jooks insteadada sliotar."

Cat

adj.

Having undesirable or negative qualities.

"Dat wan I stawled last night was cat, she gave me stubble rash an' all, feck dat boy!"

[syn: Manky]

Cayer

n.

An automobile.

"I'll give ye wan-tirty for dat deddly dinky boy, I loves dat cayer so I does."

Cewlar (Offa de)

n.

A refrigeration unit.

*"Giz a layarge bohhel offa de cewlar boy, an'
somma dat diet shyte for me lack."*

Cheeser

n.

A skimming of the fingers in a whipping motion
over an unsuspecting friend's arse.

*"Yeeeaaaoooowwww!!! Ye feckin cuncha, whatcha
give me a cheeser for? Now I'm gonna hafta bayte
de feckin' head offa ye!"*

Chynie(s)

n.

Small spherical pieces made of marble, glass or
other solid substance, used as a plaything by
children; or, in the plural, a child's game played
with chynies.

*"I got some dose o' piles boy. Dey were like a big
bag a chynies!"*

[syn: Mebs]

Chippur (de)

n.

A fish and chip establishment.

"I fell on me face de udder night on de way home from de chippur, an' I et me own eye tinkin' it was a pickled egg..."

Conkers

n.

A game played with horse chestnuts dangling from strings. Players strike each other's chestnuts to smash them.

"Fancy a game of conkers boy, I found a ginormous one down de Payples' Park!"

An extremely childish term for testicles.

"I got a kick in the conkers and went down like a sack of spuds."

Craic

v.

General Irish word for fun.

[syn: Buzz]

Crubeens

n.

A delicacy eaten in Waterford. Quite simply, pigs trotters.

"I loves suckin' de toes offa dem crubeens boy, dey remind me of me lack's chilblains."

Cuncha (ye)

n.

A name given to someone who does something cruel or nasty.

"Did you just layve off boy? Watcha do dat for ye cuncha!"

Cut

n.

Non stylish.

"Look at de cut of yer wan. She haves a haircut like yer wan offa Bosco."

[syn: State]

14

D

Das De Why

exp.

That is just the way things are.

Faydur: "Get up to yer room an' don't come down 'till I tell ye, ye little nuitna…"
Mickey: "But why Daddy?"
Faydur: "Das de why!"

Daw

n.

A stupid idiot.

"Yer tellin' me ye forgot to pull down your skunders before going for a shtyte? Yer some feckin daw boy!"

[syn: Eejit, Nuitna]

Dawdlin
adv.

The act of time wasting.

*"Give up de dawdlin' in dayer will ye boy.
Remember dat more den tree shakes is a sin..."*

Deddly
adj.

Brilliant.

"Dat ting over dayer is deddly ihinnit boy!"

Déise (up de)
n.

The land encompassing all of County Waterford
and arguably some land in surrounding counties.
Waterford hurling fans utter this word
uncontrollably during matches as follows:

"Up de Deise boy! Good man boy!"

Diddly

n.

A collection club e.g. a Christmas savings club.

"Ye better gimme all of de diddly money now love or I'll folly ye to de pub layter on and tell all de lads about yer dinky collection!"

Diddies

n.

Childish term for the mammary glands or breasts.

"Yer wan haves some pair of diddies boy."

Dig

v.

A blow with the fist.

"I gave yer man some dig in de head for saying I haves a rasher arse."

[syn: Box]

Dinky

n.

A miniature cayer.

*"Right boy, you get de peteral an' de matches, an'
I'll bring de dinkies and de ramp. Den we'll fire
dem at a few yungwans passin' by and maybe
dey'll g'waffwit us!"*

Dilisk

n.

An "edible" dried seaweed that is always gritty
and extremely salty.

*Johnny: "Jaynee mack boy I loves de auld bit a
dilisk in a bread and buttdur sangwich, specially
when it's sandy, reminds me of when I used to ayte
chewin' gum offa de ground boy..."*

*Mickey: "Gway boy, tis seaweed boy, they used ate
dat durin' de famine but I'd ate me conkers first if
ye gave it to me now."*

Dogs-End (the)

n.

The last morsel of any consumable substance.

"Givus de dogs-end of dat scallop boy, ye big mayner."

Doo-be

adv.

Being of a certain state.

"Dat butcher's hands doo-be manky, and it ihint from de mayte nayder!"

Doonchy

adj.

Extremely small. Mass challenged.

Yer wan last night had deese doonchy diddies boy! Dey looked like tablets on an ironin' board boy!

[syn: Tweenchy]

Dose

n.

A serious bout.

"I got some dose of de scutters after de big bollix said, 'Do ye want yer go boy?'"

Double Bumbeller

n.

A two litre bottle of cider.

"Hey yungfella, wud ye go in an' get us a few double bumbellers? Yer man in de offy tinks I'm drunk an' I've only lurried back tree or fower so far."

Drownded

n.

To be soaked through to the skin.

"I was only saturated after he trew his pint on me de udder night, I was drownded goin' home… an' all I did was tell him he haves bigger diddies den me. He'll be stawlin the back of his hand for de next month now."

Duck (on de)

v.

To miss class at school without permission.

"Let's go on de duck and head dowen towen boy, I need to get a new topper for me pencil boy."

[syn: Mitch]

Duff (up de)

adj.

To be pregnant.

"I told yer wan dat being up de duff suited her. I was mortified when I found out she was just heavy boned."

[syn: Pole]

E

Et

v.

The act of ingestion, past tense.

"I et a fayde o' blaas for me lunch so I cuddent ayte me dinner, so' den me muddur et de feckin' head offa me."

Eejit

v.

A word, used by Irish people in general, to describe a foolish person. Often prefixed with the word feckin'. E.g.

"Ye feckin' eejit!"

[syn: Nuitna, Daw]

F

Fanny

n.

(See Gowl)

Fayde

n.

A large quantity of any given edible item.

"Ye outdone yerself dis time mammy. Dat was some fayde o'graysey scallops ye got from de chippur."

Faydur

n.

Male parent.

"Me Faydur gave me some root in de hole, after I told him I spent all his feckin dole."

Folly (to)

v.

To go in pursuit of; to chase.

"Dat yungwan follied me home after school again yesterday lads! She's as odd as me arse!"

NOTE: Not to be confused with the road connecting Ballytruckle and Grange.

Foundaghee

n.

Where all de owl' fellas in de city useta work.

"I stawled me lack, by de foundaghee wall…"

Note: The rolling rrr often heard in Waterford dialect (e.g. Girl = Gerhel), are probably due to French influence as are the following…

Frenchies

n.

(See Jonnies)

G

Galavantin'

v.

An excursion of sorts, generally a time occupied with horse play.

"Ye better get dat galavantin' out of yer system before ye get married boy, de only galavantin' you'll be doin den is to de odd match an' das owny if yer lucky like me…"

Gallybander

n.

A home made slingshot/catapult, made out of a wire coat hanger and a mixed array of elastic bands, or simply an elastic band.

"I got a slap in de eye offa copper bullet fired from me brudder's gallybander and I couldn't see me mebs for a week!"

Gallybandered

adj.

An intoxicated state after excessive consumption of alcoholic beverages.

"Jeepers, I'm gallybandered after doze fifteen layarge bottles o' cider boy."

[syn: Locked, Skuttered, Rats]

Gawk

v.

To stare.

"What are ye gawkin' at boy, do ye want yer go boy, I'll bayte de feckin' head offa ye!"

Geatch

n.

An unusual stride or walk.

"Take a look at the geatch on yer man, he must have an irey hole."

Gee

n.

A childish term for the vagina. Often used in the delivery of a sarcastic response.

"Will I g'waffwit yer brudder? I will in me gee boy."

[syn: Fanny, Gowl, Vanny]

Gerhel

n.

Girl, as spoken in the old Waterford dialect.

Gilly Goolies

n.

(See Gushy)

Ginormous

n.

Huge.

"Did ye see de ginormous diddies on yer man's lack. He's wan lucky sucker!"

Glass (de)

n.

Waterford's famous crystal factory.

"College me bollix, me faydur and nine uncles said dey'd get me into de Glass!"

G'luck

exp.

(See All de best)

Go (yer)

v.

Hand to hand combat.

"Do ya want yer go boy? I'll give ye a baytin' by de bull-post at hallef past 4! Don't be late or I'll get worried about ye!"

Gob

n.
General Irish term for mouth.

"Shut yer gob or I'll shut it for ye!"

[syn: Cake Hole]

Goody

n.

A local "dish" made with bread and hot milk.

Gowl

n.

Childish name for the vagina. Often used in the description of a practical joker or the act of horse play.

"Would you ever give up de gowlin' for feck sake ye little gowlbag."

[syn: Fanny, Gee, Vanny]

Grand job

adj.

All right.

"Grand job, I'll be over fifteen minutes earlier with yer crusty blaas in future so."

G'waffwit, to
v.

To date or court.

"See dat fella over dayer? He wantsta know if yed g'waffwit me."

Gushy
n.

Collective term for the testicles and penis.

"Look at yer man over dayer scratchin' his gushy, the dirty guyer."

Guyer (as gaeilge = gadhar)
n.

Useless dog. Person of poor character.

"De bollix dat stole me fone is some guyer"

G'way (boy)
exp.

Go away. Get out of it.

"Ye did in yer arse stawl her? Would ye g'way boy!!!"

H

Hames

v.

A complete mess.

"He made a hames of me vasectomy boy, now I don't know whedder I'm comin' or goin'."

[syn: Bollixed it up]

Happent

adv.

To have not.

Teacher: *"Mickey, could you state Boyle's law for de class?"*

Mickey: *"Nah boy, I happent a clue boy!"*

31

Hiden

n.

(see Baytin')

Headaball / Head-de-ball

n.

A foolish person that often does the unexpected.

"Yer man over dayer is some headaball. I heard him layve off a ripper and den he wafted it at everywan!"

Hole

n.

The anus.

"When I get home I'm going to tear me lack's knickers off cos' dayer cuttin' de hole offa me."

Hoppmans

n.

A Déise beer brewed and consumed at the side of the Kay River (River Suir).

"I was in de feckin' rats on de kay after twellev pints a Hoppmans boy!

Horrors (in de)

adj.

Extremely drunk.

"I was in de horrors last night boy. I ended up puukin me guts up in some owl wan's wheelie bin on de way home boy."

[syn: Gallybandered, Ossified, Rat Arsed]

I

Illuminous

n

A descriptive term for the level of brightness produced by coloured highlighter pens.

"Givuss dat illuminous pink marker boy, I want to draw a bit of luncheon sausage onto me blaa."

Ire (pronounced eye-er)

n

A rash induced by rubbing together of skin and wet clothing e.g. on the inner thighs.

"Yer man must have ire under his arms, his pants are so far up his hole!"

[syn: chaffing]

J

Jaynee Mack (boy)

exp.

An expression of wonder.

"Jaynee mack boy, yer wan gave me a right seein tew last night, so she did!"

Jacks

n.

A room containing a toilet.

Mudder: *"Where are ye Johnny?"*

Johnny: *"I'm up in de jacks, I've a dose of de scutters after dat fayde o' scallops I had last night!"*

Jibber

n.

A coward.

"Yer man is some jibber boy... he should have saved the feckin' ball with his face!"

Jocks

n.

An undergarment that covers the body from the waist no further than to the thighs.

"Will ye get me a few new pairs of jocks girl. Deese wans are cuttin de hole of me, an' I might aswell be flossin' me crack".

[syn: Skundies]

Jonah

n.

A person with whom bad luck is associated. A jinx.

"Yer some Jonah! Every time ye go to a match we feckin' loose."

Jonnies (rubber)

n.

Contraceptive devices.

"I put five Euro in de rubber Jonny machine and it feckin' et it. Ah dickey, what a cock-up!"

Jooks

n.

The two male reproductive glands that produce spermatozoa and secrete androgens.

"I will in me jooks boy!"

[syn: Conkers, Mebs, Gushy, Bollix]

Karabunkle

n.

A septic boil.

"De doctor was lancin' me karabunkle when I left off. He said, it's payple like me make hees job manky! De chayke of him!"

Kay River (de)

n.

Colloquial name given to the River Suir as it passes through the Waterford City.

"I'll mate you down be de Clock Tower, at de Kay River for a few scoops layter on boy!

Knockadolly

n.

A childish game whereby the player knocks on an unsuspecting neighbour's door and then run like feck down the road.

L

Lack (de)

n.

Colloquial term for a female companion.

"Giz a layarge bohhel offa de shellef boy, anna Ritz for de lack!"

Lacksy Daisy

adj.

Lacking spirit, liveliness, or interest.

"Me yungfella won't get up off hees lazy hole to do antin', he's a good for nahin' lacksy daisy little bollix!"

Langered/Langers

adj.

(See Gallybandered)

Layber (de)

n.

The Labour Exchange.

"I meets me faayder down de layber of a Chewsday."

Layve off (to)

v.

To flatulate.

"Did you layve off dat eggy stink boy? I'm goin' tew give ye some root in de hole an' yell tink twice about layvin' off again."

Legger (to do a)

v.

To leave with hasty abandon.

"He done a legger when I told him I'd get me muddur after him."

Loand

v.

To borrow.

"Giz a loand of yer jockstrap wud ya boy, I did an accident in de last wan ye gave me a loand of!"

Locked

adj.

(See Gallybandered)

Lurry

n.

A large truck.

"Dayer is some hum offa dat slurry lurry."

To consume a copious amount swiftly.

"Whatcha lurry back me curry chip, while I was in de jacks for, ye cuncha?"

Lundrigen

n

The surname Lonergan as pronounced in the Waterford City dialect.

M

Malacky (cat's)
n.

Waste matter (i.e. poo) discharged from the body.

"That new dilisk diet is only a load of cat's malacky, I tried it and all I ended up with was skid-marks on me cacks."

[syn: Cocky, Ha Ha, Dobbers]

Malojan
adj.

Having no beneficial use or incapable of functioning usefully. Comes from the word melodeon for obvious reasons.

That feckin' flick was malojan boy, yer man put his gushy between his legs and pretended to be a yungwan. I nearly puked me ring boy."

[syn: Cat, Shyte, Bollox]

Manky
adj.

Defiled with dirt. Disgusting. Horrible.

"Stop pickin yer hole, das manky boy!"

Mayner
n.

A greedy bollix.

Mebs
n.

(See chynies)

Mickey Man
n.

A badly behaved individual.

"I'n telling yer muddur on ye for doin yer wee wee into dat squirtin gun ye little mickey man."

[syn: Fecker, Gowlbag]

Milderin' (wet)

v.

Profuse precipitation, lashing rain.

"'Twas milderin' wet de udder day boy, I was soaked through to me skundies so I was."

Moan Bag

n.

A continually vocal pessimist.

"Yer wan is some moanbag, she's always complaining about her rasher arse."

[syn: Moaney Hole]

Mortified

adj.

In a state of embarrassment.

"He caught me doing me pooly in de ditch de udder night girl. I was feckin mortified. Den to top it all off I sat on a load of nettles and stung de arse offa meself!"

Mowldies
adj.

(See Gallybandered)

Muddur (yer)
n., exp.

Female parent.

The expression 'Yer Mudder' should be reserved for special times when no other phrase can silence the opponent. Uttering this phrase often leads to several moments of stunned silence and may also lead to you getting yer go.

Drunken ruffian: *"D'ye want yer go boy?"*

Seasoned Waterfordian: *"Yer muddur!"*

Mullinavegas
n.

A village in North Waterford.

N

Nah
adv.

A refusal by use of the word nah.

Muddur: "Go and tidy your room at once boy."

Johnny: "Nah mammy, can't you see I'm lacksy daisy!"

Nayder
n.

Neither in the native Waterford dialect.

Neck (be de)
n.

A long neck bottled beverage.

"Givvus a layarge bohhel be de neck boy!"

No Bodder

exp.

Mannerly response to the phrase 'thank you' or equivalent.

"Spot on no bodder (girl) boy!"

Nob (me)

n.

Childish term for the male appendage.

"Will I g'waffwit yer sister? I will in me nob boy!"

Nuitna (pronounced newt-nah)

n.

A silly fool.

"Dat fella over dayer, scratchin his gilly goolies, is some nuitna."

[syn: Eejit, Daw]

Ocky (bum bums)

n.

Juvenile term for excrement, originating from the Irish word coc, meaning shyte (the plural being cocaí, hence ocky).

"Mammy, I got bad dose of de scutters on de way home from school, I have a right ocky bum bums now…"

Odds

n.

A small sum of money, usually requested by force.

"Any odds boy? Say no and I'll box de head offa ye!"

On de Ball

exp.

An expression of agreement.

"On de ball boy, spot on no bodder!"
[syn: Spot On]

On de Horn

exp.

To be sexually excited.

Dayer was a Deise sailor,
Dat sailed de seven seas,
He made a boat of wood an' tar,
And set out with de breeze.

America's cape was his goal,
But soon he was forlorn,
A siren's spell seduced his soul,
An' he washed up on de horn.

Ossified

n.

(See Gallybandered)

P

Pleb

n.

A person who is **not** self-actualised.

"Look at yer man with de big illuminous runners and de clown cacks, he's a right pleb ihint he?"

Pissy Bed (Piss-a-Bed)

n.

A herb of the genus Taraxacum having long tap roots and deeply notched leaves and bright yellow flowers followed by fluffy seed balls (aka Dandelion).

"I gave me lack a few pissy beds for Valentines day and she left me with a pissy bed the next morning in return!!!"

Peteral

n.

Petrol as pronounced in the Waterford dialect.

Pole (up de)

adj.

(See Duff)

Pooly(ies)

n.

Urine.

I need to urinate can be translated as:

"I'm droppin' me pooly."

Also used to describe the weather:

"'Tis like de wind dat scattered Maggie's Pooly!"

Quare

exp.

Used in conjunction with words to emphasise their importance. This term originated in Wexford but is creeping into Waterford dialect via the student population.

"Das quare bad boy, kicking him in de stones like dat for nahin."

[syn: Wicked]

Quare Wan

n.

Wife, Spouse, Partner.

"De quare wan says we have tew go tew towen for curtains. I said I'd radder a back, sack 'n' crack wax den do dat."

[syn: Lack]

R

Rasher Arse

n.

NOTE: The author does not condone the use of this extremely offensive term!

Rats (in de)

v.

(see Gallybandered)

Rat Fatten Villace

n.

An incorrectly pronounced area in the City.

Red-Iron (de)

n.

A disused railway bridge crossing the River Suir not far West of Waterford City.

"I stawled the head offa me lack down by de Red-Iron boy!"

Red Lead
n.

A large illuminous pink meat like sausage of unknown origin, otherwise known as luncheon sausage. Some say it is of a supernatural or extraterrestrial origin given its unusual colour and taste. Waterford locals believe it to be the original and best filling for blaas. One must be careful ingesting this substance as it may imbue one with superhuman abilities.

"Mammy...put red lead an' buttdur in me blaas in future, dat ham stuff is manky."

[syn: Baloney, Hillview Ham]

Root (in de hole/bollix)
n.

A very painful kicking technique used by only the most skilled Deisii. It is said that one who receives a mighty root in the hole never fully recovers either physically or mentally!

"I got a root in de hole after I wet de bed. Me lack hates when I do dat after goin' out on de lash!"

S

Sangwich (Hang)

n.

The hang sangwich is the king of all sangwiches. For those on a low budget or with a death wish they could try Red Lead as the filling instead.

Sack

n.

The scrotum.

"Bite me sack!"

Scallop

n.

A thick potato slice, coated in batter and deep fried. Available in all chippurs around Waterford. A chippur of noteworthiness will throw in a handful of chips for free.

"Do you want scallops with yer salt and vinegar boy!"

Scrawb

n., v.

A deep scratch of the skin that may cause profuse bleeding.

"See the scrawb yer wan gave me? All I said was she haves diddies like fried eggs!"

Scutter

n.

An extremely loose motion.

"I dunno what I et but I have a dose of the scutters now boy. Me poor owl' crack is sufferin."

Shat

v.

To defecate.

"I was called up on stage by dat magician fella and I nearly shat me pants boy."

"Did ye hear about de new line of womens' underwear by yer man? Dayer called Shatner pants and dayer outa dis wuhurld boy, straight from Uranus!"

Shaymus

n.

An extremely forceful knee in the quadriceps (thigh) causing paralysis.

"Dat fat bollix gave me some shaymus boy, but I managed to give him a kick in de sack before me leg went dead!"

Sheleff (Offa de)

n.

A horizontal surface for holding objects.

"Giz a layarge bohhel offa de shellef boy, anna hallef-wan for de lack."

Shellakybooky

n.

Any of numerous aquatic (Perry Winkle) or terrestrial (Snail) molluscs, typically having a spirally coiled shell.

Children's Rhyme:
"Shellaky Shellakybooky, stick out your horns and see the white lady coming to call you." – pure feckin' weird!

Shytarse

n.

A person with whom someone is totally dissatisfied.

"Yer man is some shytarse for aytin' every last wan of de crusty blaas."

Slug

v.

A large mouthful of any beverage, generally involving backwash and in extreme cases floaties.

"Giz a slug of dat lemonade boy, I tink I'm goin' to be sick…"

Sketch

n.

An unattractive human female.

"Dat wan you stawled was some sketch boy, she haves a face like scabby arse!"

Skuttered

n.

(See Gallybandered)

Skunders/Skundies

n.

(See Jocks)

Skint

n.

To be without money.

"Jay boy, dat dirty guyer lost me a fortune last night out at de races boy. I'm feckin' skint so I am…"

Snot Rag

n.

An apparatus used to wipe de snot of an owl fella's nose. A handkerchief.

"Hab anywan a loand ob an owl snot rag dat I can wibe be dose with? I promise it won't be tew crusty when ye get it back obba be."

Spot On
exp.

See "On de ball"

Stawl
v.

The act of caressing with the lips.

"I stawled de head offa yer wan last night behind de Glass boy, tomorrow I'm going for the 21 and maybe even the square."

"Did ye get de stawl offa yer wan at de back of de Regina boy?"

[syn: G'waffwit, Shift]

T

Taw
n.

A large chynie.

[syn: Chynies, Mebs]

Timber (to give)
v.

To cause intentional bodily harm with a wooden implement, such as a hurley.

"Anwell we'll win against dem langers boy, and if we don't shurr we'll give 'em some timber anyhow!"

Topper
n.

A pencil sharpener.

"Can I have a loand of yer topper boy? De led in me pencil is all blunted boy."

Tweenchy
adj.

(See Doonchy)

Trun
v.

To fling or cast with a certain whirling motion of the arm.

"I trun a dig at him but he bursted me with hees hurley before I even connected."

U

Udder

n.

Not the same item.

"You've been milking dat udder for ages. Wud ye ever move to de udder udder wud ye boy?"

V

Vee (de)

v.

A scenic valley in the Knockmealdown mountain range.

"Daddy, brin' us up to de vee, so we can fire our gallybanders at dem sheep again.'

Vamp

v.

To Kick.

"I gave yer man a good owl fashioned vamp up in de arse!"

[syn: Root]

Vanny

v.

The Vagina.

Johnny: *"In school today, I learnt where babies come from mammy an' it begins with a 'V'"*

Muddur: *"Oh yeah? Where's dat Johnny?"*

Johnny: *"De Vanny!"*

[syn: Gowl, Gee, Fanny]

Wahent

adv.

A form of denial.

"It wahent me I swear boy. 'Twas de wan armed man boy!"

Wan

n

The number one, as in: "wan, tew, tree, fower…"
An adult human female.

"See dat ride of a wan over there? De udder night I went over tew her an' said 'Well girl boy, would ye g'waffwit me?' An' she told me to go buttdur me arse and slide dowen a rainbow, imagine dat boy! de chake of it."

Well (boy)

exp.

An expression of greeting; can be used in conjunction with boy and girl depending on the sex of the addressee.

"Well boy, 'ow's de lack?"

Wee Wee

n.

Urine.

"Stop de bus we want a wee wee..." is an old tour bus favourite, sung to the tune of Glory, Glory Hallelujah.

Whang

v.

To detect or perceive, as if by the sense of smell.

"Jaynee boy, what a whang, did you just layve off ye dirty bollix? A rat must have crawled up yer hole and died!"

[syn: Layve off]

Wicked

n.

A term used mostly in West Waterford to highlight something of noteworthiness.

"Dem pints lasht night were wicked tayshty, but now I'm fartin' like a trouper boy!"

[syn: Quare]

Wilnots

n.

Bum fluff.

"Dem feckin wilnots just will not come off boy!"

X-scallybur

n.

A night club, long since gone, renowned for its favour with more mature Waterford ladies, and also de yungfellas tryin' tew g'waffwit dem.

Y

Yer Stink
exp.

A phrase to describe someone with chronic flatulence.

"Would ye g'way boy, yer stink! You'd wanna get dat seen tew quick boy!"

Yungwan
n.

A young woman.

Yungfella: *"Yungwan, haves ye a match?"*
Yungwan: *"Yeah, yer head an' me arse!"*

Yungfella
n.

A young man.

"Hey yungfella? Go over dayer and ask dat yungwan if she'll g'waffit me!"

Z

Zee End

(as the Hŭguenŏts would have said it)

What have we learnt?

At dis stage ye should be fluent in de art of Waterford slang boy! So try de followin' tew test yer abilities boy (answers on de following page if ye want tew chayte):

1. What is a 'blaa'?
a) A bap (it's not a feckin' bap!)
b) A bit of useless information
c) A bread product, unique to Waterford

2. What is a 'lack'?
a) A deficit in something
b) A lazy bollix
c) A girlfriend

3. What does the term 'cannt' mean?
a) To lose a ball over a wall or ditch
b) To fail miserably
c) To arse about

4. What does the term 'cat' mean?
a) A Kilkenny hurler
b) A small agile animal of the feline variety
c) Something that is extremely bad

5. What are 'chynies'?
a) Marbles
b) Oriental people
c) An uppercut

6. What is a 'gallybander'?
a) A person who plays in a band on a boat
b) A sling shot / catapult
c) A testicle

7) What does 'on de ball' mean?
a) Good positional sense in soccer
b) To use an exercise ball during labour
c) A phrase used to agree with someone

8) What are 'scallops'?
a) A type of fish
b) Deep friend potato slices in batter
c) Ugly yungwans

9) What is a 'shellakybooky'?
a) A crusty snot
b) A snail
c) A rugby player

10) If someone asks you for 'yer go' what do they want you to do?
a) Take your turn
b) Play conkers with them
c) Fight them

If you answered all 10 right you are a true Deisii. If not den ye can rayde de book again or chayte by raydin deese boy!

Answers: 1c, 2c, 3a, 4c, 5a, 6b, 7c, 8b, 9b, 10c

About the Author

De auter of dis book is a yungfella called Cian "Wellboy" Foley. Wellboy is a proud Déise yungfella and as such he enjoys de bit of red lead in his blaas and he loves to wash them down with few layarge bohhels. Dayers nahin he likes better den to go spinnin around de Déise with de quaar wan and his little sprogs, visitin' all de sights on offer; de beaches, de mountains, de castles and all de udder historic stuff.

Wellboy set up a community website called UpTheDeise.com a few years ago in order dat Waterford's culture, history and beauty be celebrated by de payple of Waterford, home and abroad. The goal of de site is to generate a bit of blaa pride and have an owl craic at de same time.

Anyway, enough of de owl shyte. The auter would like to tank you for buyin' dis book and hopes dat you enjoyed it as he spent at layste wan whole hour puttin' it all togedder.

You can contact de auter at dis email address boy: wellboy@upthedeise.com

About UpTheDeise.com

UpTheDeise.com is Waterford's number one community website. It was created for the people of Waterford, Ireland and beyond as an outlet for people to share their experiences of the Deise and have a bit of craic at the same time.

The crest on the site symbolises unity between East and West Waterford signified by Ardmore and Reginald's Tower linked by the mountains in between. The three ships in an offensive formation symbolise Waterford's legendary defence over the years and its new go-get-them attitude.

There are lots of things to explore on UpTheDeise.com and there are many interactive parts to the site so why not explore it and try some of the following services:

- The Discussion Forum is a great place to share your views on Waterford issues, sport etc.

- You can upload and view hundreds of Waterford pictures in the Gallery

- You can download mp3s, check out jokes etc. in the craic section.

- The tourism and history section gives some details on points of interest in the Deise.

- You can read user articles and letters published by users in the Blogs section.

- You can buy Waterford merchandise in the online shop.

- You can advertise your services

- You can have an owl craic!

www.UpTheDeise.com

for all your Waterford wants and Déise desires...

About Waterford

 Waterford is a fantastic county in South East Ireland with an amazing history, spectacular scenery, and a unique culture. Waterford's history spans many thousands of years, Waterford City being Ireland's oldest city and Old Parish near the beautiful Ardmore being the oldest Christian parish in the country, pre-dating even St. Patrick. There are Castles, Historic Buildings, Dolmens, and Ogham stones dotted around the county also. Some historic characters of note are: TF Meagher, one of the nine fine Irishmen, who conceived and first raised the Irish flag in Waterford; Robert Boyle, internationally known as the father of chemistry; Luke Wadding, who set up St. Patrick's day as a feast day; and Edmund Rice, founder of the Christian Brothers. There are simply too many to mention here.

Waterford also boasts some spectacular scenery such as: the world class Corrie lakes in the Comeragh mountains (Coumshingaun and Crotty's lake); the Towers loop walk in Ballysaggartmore (a totally magical experience); 40+ beaches on its 70 mile, geologically unique, copper coast line; and some amazing walks through woods and marshes. It has to be experienced to be believed!

Finally, it has a unique culture where people are always up for a bit of craic (joking about). They speak their own language, as is evident by the slang in this book. It also boasts a unique cuisine in the form of Blaas, Goody, Dilisk and Crubeens for example. All in all, Waterford is an amazing place to live and the quality of life here is just fantastic boy.

Some Waterford Facts:

- Waterford City is Ireland's Oldest City
- Old Parish near Ardmore is Ireland's oldest Christian parish, dating back to before St. Patrick's time. It is located near Ardmore, which is the site of a beautiful round tower in a magnificent setting with breathtaking coastal views.
- The Christian Brothers' were founded in Waterford by Blessed Edmund Ignatius Rice in 1802
- Waterford city is the only city where the Protestant and Catholic Cathedrals were built by the same man, John Roberts. The Roman Catholic Cathedral is the oldest in Ireland

- The Irish Flag was flown for the very first time in Waterford City on the 7th of March 1848 at 33 the Mall and was conceived by Waterford and Irish legend, TF Meagher.
- Waterford has had many names, Vadre Fjord, Port Láirge, Cuan-na-Grian, Glean-na-nGleodh, Urbs Intacta, Decies, Déise
- Reginald's Tower is the oldest urban medieval monument in Ireland and is one of 6 towers still standing in Waterford as part of the old city walls after 1000 years
- The phrase By Hook or By Crooke originated here from the place names Hook and Crooke when Cromwell vowed that his armies would take Waterford 'by Hook or by Crooke'. He never did.
- The first Governor of New Zealand was Waterford born William Hobson
- Born and reared in Lismore Castle, Co. Waterford, Robert Boyle is hailed as the Father of Chemistry and is most famous for Boyle's Law
- ETS Walton was the first man to split the atom and the only Irish man to win the Nobel Prize for Science!
- The bacon curing process (bacon / rashers) was invented in Waterford

- Waterford has approximately 40 beautiful beaches dotted along its beautiful copper coast. The copper coast is geologically unique, with spectacular views and points of interest such as the pipes of baidhb and the old copper mines.

- The Most significant Viking find in recent times was discovered in Woodstown along the river Suir, it has been called the Pompeii of Europe and is of major international significance

- There are Dolmens, Megalithic tombs, Cairns, Ogham Stones, standing stones and ruins all around the county

- William Vincent Wallace probably the greatest opera composer and organist the country has ever produced (his works include, Maritana, the opera).

- The Metal Man is a unique point of interest on Newtown head, West of Tramore Bay (which is one of the finest beaches in the country)

- It is one of only 5 counties in Ireland with a Gaeltacht, An Rinn or Ring, with around 1000 native Irish speakers. It is a very beautiful part of the county.

- There are some impressive remains of monasteries in the City, once called "Little Rome" due to the sheer number of churches and monasteries etc.

- Towers of Ballysaggartmore, West of Lismore, is a magical site with a beautiful woodland walk, suitable for family excursions. The gates of grandeur and the entrance gate were built before they ran out of money. If you visit make sure you search for the Waterfall.

- Dromana Gate, stands along the Villierstown-Cappoquinn road. It is the only Hindu-gothic building in Ireland

- Mt. Mellary is an impressive monastery in a beautiful setting on the Vee drive.

- Sean Kelly, a cyclist from Rathgormack, County Waterford, is ranked in the top 10 cyclists of all time. He is in good company with other famous Waterford sports people such as Percy Kirwan, John Treacy, Jim Beglin, Paddy Coad, Alfie Hale, John O'Shea, John Keane and Philly Grimes.

- Coumshingaun, a corrie lake in the Comeragh mountains, is said to be the finest glacial lake in Europe.

- Many international businesses started in Waterford, including Ryan Air, Jacobs biscuits and Grubb telescopes.

- Luke Wadding, a Friar from Greyfriars of Waterford, set up St. Patrick's day.

About Time
Dis Book Ended Boy

www.UpTheDeise.com
"For all your Waterford Wants and Deise Desires"